The True God Workbook

by
R. S. "Bud" Miller, D.D.
Publisher
Betty Miller, D.M.
Author

www.BibleResources.org

Overcoming Life Series

Christ Unlimited — P.O. Box 850 — Dewey, AZ 86327   USA

Unless otherwise indicated, all Scripture quotations are taken from the <u>King James Version of the Holy Bible</u> (KJV).

<u>Overcoming Life Series</u>

<u>The True God Workbook</u>

ISBN 1-57149-003-5

Copyright © 1995-2013

R. S. "Bud" and Betty Miller

P. O. Box 850

Dewey, Arizona 86327

Published by

Christ Unlimited Publishing

P. O. Box 850

Dewey, Arizona 86327

Publisher: Pastor R. S. "Bud" Miller

Printed in the United States of America.

Contents

Personal Introduction

A lack of education will not hinder anyone from taking this course, and a doctor's degree will not help. However, one requirement that is necessary for this course to benefit the student is a <u>total commitment</u> to God. The Holy Spirit is our teacher, and we can learn if we come to God as little children. Being hungry to know God is a necessary prerequisite in order for this course to be of help.

If any of us are to receive truth, we must seek God, who is truth, with our whole hearts. We must seek Jesus first, then the knowledge of His Word will be revealed to us. Therefore, we want to emphasize once again the need to become as "a little child" in our approach to learning God's Word (Matt. 18:1-4; Jer. 29:13).

We need to come humbly before God, asking Him to remove any "know-it-all" attitudes, in order to be teachable. By laying down everything we thought we knew, we give God a chance to correct things we have believed that were wrong. Then we can begin to live the overcoming lives that God intended for His children to experience.

This course, the <u>Overcoming Life Series</u>, is made up of nine books and workbooks taken from our first published book, <u>How To Overcome Through the Christ Unlimited</u>. That book, given to us under the anointing of the Holy Spirit, covers most of the basic things a Christian needs to know to get started on a victorious, overcoming walk with the Lord.

We have purposely kept this course simple for the average Christian who needs help in understanding how to study the Word and how to sort out principles and concepts when he, or she, reads the Bible; however, it also is for the seminary student. In addition, it is designed for students who desire to use it as a correspondence course. They can learn from it, even if they are totally alone and without a human teacher. The Holy Spirit always is there to teach us as we study about His Word.

On the other hand, groups with a teacher, or moderator, also can use this course to advantage. Our prayer is that however this course is taken, each student will complete it a different person and be conformed more into the image of Christ our Lord.

Bud and Betty Miller

The True God Workbook
"God's Nature and Character"

Christ Unlimited — P.O. Box 850 — Dewey, AZ 86327   USA

The True God Workbook
"God's Nature and Character"
Expository Introduction

[Author's Note: This workbook in the Overcoming Life Series is based on the book The True God. There are nine books and workbooks in this series. Lessons have supplementary material in addition to the books. The answers are provided at the end of the workbook and do not have to be the exact wording in many cases. The student simply needs to make sure that he has caught the concept or principle from the Word of God.]

This course is designed to help Christians study the Word of God, and while so doing, find out how to live a victorious Christian life. Simply becoming a Christian unfortunately does not guarantee that a person will live a victorious life. Through these teachings, lessons, outlines, and quizzes, we are trying to show students the principles that will make the difference between being defeated Christians or Christians victorious in Christ.

In this workbook, we are going to look at the nature and character of God. If a Christian really does not know the true nature of God and who He is, he will not know the reality of Jesus and cannot try to live as Jesus did while here on earth.

Even within the ranks of those truly born again, the way people view God will vary, because each person has been exposed to a different "picture" of God. Many times, our ideas of God are based on things we have learned or decided about the main male authority figures in our lives as children.

If a person's father was permissive, he may see God that way.

If his father was an abuser, he may tend to see God as harsh, unloving, and judgmental.

Descriptions of God will vary according to:

1. The knowledge a person has of God personally

2. The knowledge a person has of His Word

3. The knowledge a person has of God based on what others have told that person about Him

4. The experiences a person has had with those in authority and with those who present themselves as servants of God

Christians are reflections of God's nature and character through their own lifestyles when they are obeying God. Many times, however, the life of a Christian does not give the world a true picture of the heavenly Father but gives Him a "bad name" because Christians do not always obey God and walk by His principles.

Obviously, our experiences do not really tell us what God is like and should not be used as a basis on which to form our opinions of God. Yet, many times, these things are what mold the way people think of God. The fact is that our experiences are not the truth by which God is to be measured. The truth about God is found in His Word, and our experiences should be measured by the Bible.

As Christians mature, our understanding and knowledge of God changes. God Himself never changes. He is the same yesterday, today, and forever (Mal. 3:6; Heb. 13:8). However, the "picture" or understanding that each Christian has of the Father should become clearer and more accurate as each person matures spiritually. God does not change; so we are the ones who must change.

But we all, with open face beholding as in a glass the glory of the Lord, are changed into the same image from glory to glory, even as by the Spirit of the Lord.

2 Corinthians 3:18

As we change through knowing God better, the things we used to believe change. Once we really know God, no one will be able to tell us false things about Him and have us believe them.

The <u>first</u> discovery we need to make about God is this:

<u>There is only one God and only one way to Heaven</u>, although God is represented in three personalities: Father, Son, and Holy Spirit.

More and more in this century, people either say there is no God or they say there are many ways to get to Him; these are based on man's traditions, or works. Neither of these alternatives are found in the Bible; the only written source we have for information about God. Proverbs 16:25 says:

There is a way that seemeth right unto a man, but the end thereof are the ways of death.

Some of the wrong ideas (the "ways that seem right") that people have about God include the following ideas that God is:

*A "force" that set everything in motion, but is not a personality.

*Nature itself. In other words, "God" is in everything alike — the planet, flowers, trees, birds, animals, and man.

The truth is that these things are <u>not</u> God, but His creations. Called <u>pantheism</u>, this philosophy, theory, or idea evolves into the worship of nature. They were doing that in ancient times, as Paul writes in **Romans 1**.

Some present-day ecologists have embraced this theology, and they have elevated God's creatures and His creation above man's needs.

Certainly God is interested in caring for His creation. This fact was demonstrated in the saving of all animal flesh by placing them in the ark with Noah when the earth was destroyed by the flood of waters due to man's sin.

God is concerned about preserving our planet and its animals, as well as its environment. But most of the ecology groups are going about "saving the earth" in the wrong manner.

First, we must see what the problem truly is that is causing the destruction of our earth and its inhabitants. That <u>problem</u> is sin.

Animals and the environment are being abused because of man's greed, wastefulness, selfishness, and abusiveness. Men's hearts must be changed to correct the problem.

Changing only the circumstances related to the problem can create other problems. An example is rescuing a few animals, while eliminating the jobs of many people.

As Christians, we are commanded to have dominion over the earth and animal kingdom. If we exercise dominion properly, according to God's Word and by His nature, the animals and our environment will be cared for by His love and instruction.

And God blessed them, and God said unto them, Be fruitful, and multiply, and replenish the earth, and subdue it: and have dominion over the fish of the sea, and over the fowl of the air, and over every living thing that moveth upon the earth.

Genesis 1:28

Proverbs 12:10 says:

A righteous man regardeth the life of his beast; but the tender mercies of the wicked are cruel.

Many environmentalists have elevated the animal kingdom to be equal with mankind, which is not right. Animals are not spiritual beings, having only souls and bodies. God's crowning creation was man, who was created in His image (Gen. 1:26).

Other Misconceptions About God

Other ways people see God are as:

*A gray-haired and gray-bearded old man sitting on a throne watching and waiting to hit us over the head when we make mistakes.

*A tyrant who is the cause of all catastrophes, sicknesses, poverty, and other terrible things in our lives. He is trying to "teach us a lesson," these people say. Actually, they have the character of God mixed up with the nature of the devil! God only allows things to happen when His grace and mercy have been trampled on past the point when He can withhold judgment and be just.

The Bible reveals that the way to see God is through Jesus (John 14:6). God came to earth in the physical form of Jesus (John 6:46-51). Jesus was all-God, and yet all-man; a mystery we will not be able to truly understand until we reach Heaven. The largest amount of information concerning the life of Jesus on earth is found in the gospels: Matthew, Mark, Luke, and John. In the reports we are given by those first-hand witnesses of His life, we will never find that He did any wicked thing, that He ever turned away any who came to Him for healing, or that He did anything of His own will. Everything He did was what He saw the Father do (John 5:19).

Even then, the Christian had to "see" Jesus with spiritual eyes. Many of those who saw Him literally in the flesh when He was on earth did not receive Him, because He did not fit the traditions they had developed about Messiah. They looked at Him with eyes of flesh, not spiritual eyes. Good examples of seeing in the spirit are Simeon and Anna, the only two people we are told about in the Bible who recognized Jesus solely through witnesses in their spirits when He was a baby (Luke 2:25-38). The shepherds at His birth were told by angels, and the wise men followed the sign of a star. However, Simeon and Anna were given no signs or no visions of angels. They knew Him in their spirits.

So we can see that the best way to see God is through Jesus, after we receive Him in our hearts. Then we are to grow in Him in order to become like Him. We not only are "born again" with a new Father, but within us is the potential to become like His first-born Son, Jesus. The most important factor after being reborn is to keep the right heart attitude before the Father. To facilitate this and grow in God, we must daily: 1) pray, 2) study God's Word, and 3) fellowship with like believers.

Some things that will hinder our seeing Jesus are: being disobedient, being rebellious (unsubmissive and unyielding), having wrong attitudes toward others and wrong ideas about God, and spending too much time with unbelievers. Too much time spent with those not in the faith, or even with Christians who have doubt and unbelief, can cause us to lose our own faith in God.

If our ideas about God are wrong, we will have difficulty obeying Him and fellowshipping with Him. Our understanding of four main concepts in life will cause us to walk in a victorious Christian life or a defeated one. Those four things are our concepts of God, of Satan, of ourselves, and of others. False ideas in any of these areas will hinder us from living a victorious life.

Obviously, our concepts of God are important, but it may not be as clear why it also is necessary to understand some things about the devil. We need to know that when God created Lucifer, he was beautiful and perfect until pride, self-will, and rebellion were found in him (Ezk. 28:12-19). Apparently the most beautiful being God had created, Lucifer brought war to Heaven and was cast out with a third of the angels (Rev. 12:3,4). He became the one responsible for all of the evil in the world — not God (Isa. 14:12-17)!

When God placed Adam and Eve on the earth, Satan had no power over either of them. Only when they disobeyed God's specific commandment (Gen. 2:16,17) did Satan become their master. Sin entered the world. When we disobey and rebel, we are in agreement with the enemy. Many times, we do not see the sin in our lives that is allowing the devil to master us. Sin is missing the mark of being like God.

There are several false concepts that people believe about the devil. These include:

1. That he is a mythological character
2. That he has no power over Christians (Actually, he has no authority, but he has all the power we allow him to have.)
3. That he is more powerful than he is, which leads to fearing him instead of God

It is necessary to have spiritual revelation in three important areas to be victorious. We need to know:

*Who God is (His nature and character)

*Who we are without Him

*Who we are in Him, or rather, who He is in us.

Looking at the first revelation of knowing God, we must examine the character or nature of God to be able to understand Him and how He operates.

Only Divine Love Is Complete Love

The major descriptive attribute, or characteristic, of God in Scripture is His love (1 John 4:7,8; Matt. 22:36-40; John 14:15, 15:9-12). God's whole nature and character is generally summed up in this one encompassing character description — love! The Apostle Paul wrote that nothing can separate us from the love of God (Rom. 8:38,39).

The word <u>love</u> in our society as used today is not at all the meaning of God's love. Let's look at the different meanings of this word <u>love</u> as used in the New Testament.

Four Greek words are translated as <u>love</u> in English, but only three of them are used in Scripture.[1] They are:

<u>Agapao</u> or <u>agape</u>, "divine love" or "love of God."

<u>Phileo</u>, strong tender affection, which is used for friendships or relationships.

<u>Philadelphia</u>, which is brotherly love or family love, and combines <u>phileo</u> (to love) with <u>adelphos</u> (brotherly love).

<u>Eros</u>, which means sexual love, and from which we get the English word such as "erotic."

Nothing in the New Testament deals with "erotic" love.

<u>Agape</u> is the kind of love Christians need to walk in to be victorious and only God can provide this kind of love for His followers.[2]

God's love is a supernatural love, because it is a sacrificial love which demands that we love our enemies and even do good to them that hate us (Matt. 5:44). Only God's <u>agape</u> love is sufficient for this task.

Isaiah 9:6 says:

For unto us a child is born, unto us a son is given: and the government shall be upon his shoulder: and his name shall be called Wonderful, Counsellor, the mighty God, the everlasting Father, the Prince of Peace.

This scripture is descriptive of the many other facets of God's nature and different attributes which include:[3]

*Mercy (Ps. 136; Heb. 4:15-16) — God stooped down to man's level through Jesus, so He understands our plight (Heb. 4:15-16).

For we have not an high priest which cannot be touched with the feeling of our infirmities; but was in all points tempted like as we are, yet without sin. Let us therefore come boldly unto the throne of grace, that we may obtain mercy and find grace to help in time of need.

God's mercy endures forever (Ps. 136). Mercy is the disposition to pardon a crime that deserves punishment. We all deserve Hell. Instead, through God's mercy, we receive Heaven if we accept Jesus, the only Way to salvation (John 10:9). Matthew 5:7 says that the merciful are blessed and will receive mercy. We can store up mercy for our time of need by being merciful to others who are fallen.

*Goodness (Isa. 9:6; Ps.31:19; John 14:14; Acts 10:38; James 1:17) — a reflection of Jesus being a wonderful person. Isaiah 9:6 said that Jesus' name "would be called Wonderful." A name reveals something about a person or a thing. When we say a person has "a good name," we are saying his name represents his character. Jesus has given us His name, which represents His character and the character of God. We can use His name by His permission. His character stands behind His name.

If ye shall ask any thing in my name, I will do it.

John 14:14

*Wisdom (1 Cor. 1:30; Eph. 1:17) — God's love directed by knowledge. Wisdom consists of the choice of the best and most valuable end and of the most appropriate means of obtaining that end. If we lack wisdom, we are to ask for it.

The Lord by wisdom hath founded the earth; by understanding hath he established the heavens.

Proverbs 3:19

O the depth of the riches both of the wisdom and knowledge of God! how unsearchable are his judgments, and his ways past finding out!

Romans 11:33

If any of you lack wisdom, let him ask of God, that giveth to all men liberally, and upbraideth not; and it shall be given him.

James 1:5

Who is a wise man and endued with knowledge among you? let him shew out of a good conversation his works with meekness of wisdom. But if ye have bitter envying and strife in your hearts, glory not, and lie not against the truth. This wisdom descendeth not from above, but is earthly, sensual, devilish. For where envying and strife is, there is confusion and every evil work. But the wisdom that is from above is first pure, then peaceable, gentle, and easy to be entreated, full of mercy and good fruits, without partiality, and without hypocrisy.

James 3:13-17

God, being all wise, has the solutions to all of our problems, and we have access to that wisdom because we are His children.

*Power — God's power is noted by the term "the mighty God" in Isaiah 9:6. The evidence of God's Being is portrayed by His power. This power, of course, is always directed toward man's highest good. It also is associated with doing the works of God (Matt. 28:18-20; Acts 1:8, 6:8; Heb. 13:8). We know that God is all-powerful.

Three terms are used in theology to describe God's power. He is omnipotent, which means unlimited power and authority (Matt. 28:18-20); omniscient, which means that God knows all things, and there is nothing we can hide from Him; and omnipresent, which means God is everywhere, in all places at the same time. (We cannot really understand any of these concepts; however, we must have the revelation that they are true of God in order to live a victorious life.) The power of God is mighty and limitless! He is the Christ Unlimited.

*Faith — Hebrews 11:3 tells us that through faith we understand the worlds were framed by the Word of God. God not only is Faith Himself, He is faithful. We, as His children, must express that faith and faithfulness also. Faith is such an important characteristic of

God that it is spoken of in scripture as a fruit, a gift, and also, as part of the spiritual armor of believers.

*Compassion — the Greek word <u>oikteiro</u> is used in **Romans 9:15**, when Paul wrote of God's compassion.

> For he saith to Moses, I will have mercy on whom I will have mercy, and I will have compassion on whom I will have compassion.

That word <u>oikteiro</u> means not only to have pity on someone but "to feel distress through the ills of others."[4]

Notice that in the same verse, Paul made a distinction between <u>mercy</u> and <u>compassion</u>. Mercy usually is extended when compassion is felt. In the Old Testament, David also made a distinction between <u>mercy</u> and <u>compassion</u>, as in **Psalm 86:15**.

> But thou, O Lord, art a God full of <u>compassion</u>, and gracious, longsuffering, and plenteous in <u>mercy</u> and truth.

When the writers of the gospels wrote of Jesus being "moved with compassion" toward those suffering with sicknesses and demon possession, they used a different word: <u>splanchnizomai</u>, which means "to be moved so strongly that one's 'inward parts' (bowels) are affected by pity."

Still a third word, <u>sumpatheo</u>, means "to suffer <u>with</u> another," which is a still stronger concept used of Christ as our High Priest in Hebrews 4:15.

Today, Christ literally "suffers" with us in our trials.

Additional Characteristics of God

Other characteristics of God include:

*<u>Truth</u> (John 14:6) — not only in the sense of not being able to lie (John 3:33), but in the sense of being absolute reality. There is nothing in Him, about Him, or that He says or does that is not absolutely accurate and real.

*<u>Justice</u> — when used about God, justice means "the perfect agreement between His nature and His acts, in which He is the standard for all men," according to <u>Vine's Dictionary</u>.[5]

Moses wrote about God's justice in Numbers:

> God is not a man, that he should lie; neither the son of man, that he should repent: hath he said, and shall he not do it? or hath he spoken, and shall he not make it good?
>
> Numbers 23:19

Abraham first spoke forth faith in the justice of God when He was interceding for the people of Sodom and Gomorrah.

> That be far from thee to do after this manner, to slay the righteous with the wicked: and that the righteous should be as

the wicked, that be far from thee: Shall not the Judge of all the earth do right?

Genesis 18:25

He is the Rock, his work is perfect: for all his ways are judgment: a God of truth and without iniquity, just and right is he.

Deuteronomy 32:4

*Severity — which is not usually one of the characteristics people consider "good" in today's permissive society. However, God's severity is upon sin and sinners who do not repent and is mentioned in the same verse as His goodness in Romans 11:21,22.

For if God spared not the natural branches, take heed lest he also spare not thee. Behold therefore the goodness and severity of God: on them which fell, severity; but toward thee, goodness, if thou continue in his goodness: otherwise thou also shalt be cut off.

*Patience — a very important characteristic for us to develop in order to live victoriously in Christ.

Now the God of patience and consolation grant you to be like-minded one toward another according to Christ Jesus.

Romans 15:5

Christ Unlimited — P.O. Box 850 — Dewey, AZ 86327   USA

Vine wrote:

"Patience perfects Christian character, James 1:4, and fellowship in the patience of Christ is therefore the condition upon which believers are to be admitted to reign with Him, 2 Tim. 2:12; Rev. 1:9. For this patience, believers are 'strengthened with all power,' Col. 1:11, 'through His Spirit in the inward man,' Eph. 3:16."[6]

*Orderliness — God is not the author of confusion, as the Apostle Paul wrote.

> For God is not the author of confusion, but of peace, as in all churches of the saints.
>
>   1 Corinthians 14:33

*Simplicity — another aspect not usually associated with God, who is more complex than anything He has created. However, in His dealings with man, His simplicity is manifested, not His complexity. Paul feared that the Corinthians' minds would be "corrupted" from the simplicity that is in Christ.

> But I fear, lest by any means, as the serpent beguiled Eve through his subtilty, so your minds should be corrupted from the simplicity that is in Christ.
>
>   2 Corinthians 11:3

*Meekness, or humility — something Jesus said of Himself. He said that He was "meek" (teachable) and "lowly" (humble) in heart (Matt. 11:29,30).

Also, the <u>fruits of the Spirit</u> (Gal. 5:22,23) are manifested in the Holy Spirit as characteristics of God. With the revelation of <u>Who God is</u>, we still need to have a revelation of <u>who we are</u>.

Concerning ourselves, we need to know that we are important to God. However, without Him, we can do nothing. We need to know He has a purpose for each of our lives and that He wants us to have esteem for ourselves <u>because of who we are in Him</u>, which is the third revelation we need.

When we see who we are without Christ, we see an ugly picture. We see hatred, meanness, murder, greed, selfishness, self-centeredness, and all of the other things the Apostle Paul listed as part of "the old man" or the "old nature," the part of man inherited from Adam (Eph. 4:22-32, 5:3-5).

The Bible says the righteousness of men without God is "as filthy rags" (Isa. 64:6). Titus 3:5,6 points out also that it is not because of any works we have done that we are saved, but only through the mercy of God. Not one person is righteous without God (Rom. 3:10). Salvation is a gift that cannot be earned.

Some people get a revelation of <u>self</u> without Christ, and it is so depressing, they commit suicide. We, as Christians, need to know who we are without Christ; but more important is who we are <u>in Christ</u>, or rather Christ in us. In Christ, we are everything He is. All we must do is receive it. The characteristics of Christ are in us through the Holy Spirit; however, just as with salvation, we must appropriate them.

Christ Unlimited — P.O. Box 850 — Dewey, AZ 86327   USA

Also, we need to see worth in others. We need to look at fellow Christians as children of God and grant them the same mercy He has granted us (Matt. 18:21-35). The faults and failures we see in others are the work of Satan, the enemy of all mankind, just as the faults and failures we find in our own selves.

To walk in victory, we need the revelation that through Christ we are overcomers of all things. Revelation 21:7 says that the overcomers shall inherit all things. Ephesians 3:16-21 tells us that we are to be filled with the fullness of God. So we see that becoming saved makes us potential overcomers, but not all who are born again learn to walk in the power and victory available to them.

The goal of all Christians, as established by God, is to be conformed to the image of Christ (Rom. 8:29). To that end, God set apostles, prophets, evangelists, teachers, and pastors in the Body of Christ (the Church) to bring us into the "measure of the fullness of Christ" (Eph. 4:11-13).

We have only one example in order to be like our Father, and that is Jesus Christ!

That gives us some idea of who God is. Who we are is a more difficult revelation to get, as we become bankrupt and hopeless without Christ (Rom. 6:23) so we cannot see ourselves clearly. The Bible truth is that who we are in Him is everything that He is. We receive His love, His gifts, and His power to overcome everything (1 John 4:4; John 1:12). We do not become divine as God is divine, but through Christ, we partake of the "divine nature." We do not become <u>as</u> God, but we can become <u>like Him</u> (made in His image).

Two scriptural tests to determine whether we are living the God-kind of love (<u>agape</u>) are these:

Do we love God first and our neighbors as ourselves (Matt. 22:36-40)? In other words do we truly love one another (John 15:9-12)?

Are we keeping God's commandments?

Are we truly obedient?

The Bible says that if we <u>truly</u> love the Father, we will obey Him (John 14:15).

Christ Unlimited — P.O. Box 850 — Dewey, AZ 86327   USA

Endnotes

[1]Vine, W. E. Vine's Expository Dictionary of Old and New Testament Words (Old Tappan: Fleming H. Revell Company, 1981), Vol. 1, pp. 154,155; Vol. 3, pp. 20-22.

Strong, James. The New Strong's Exhaustive Concordance of the Bible "Greek Dictionary of the New Testament," (Nashville: Thomas Nelson Publishers, 1984): Agapao, #25, p. 7; phileo, #5368, p. 75; and philadelphia, #5360, p. 75.

[2]A fifth word, theolo, is used once in the New Testament (Mark 12:38), but does not involve relationships. It deals with "loving" to do something, such as "to delight in" something. Strong's Greek Dictionary, #2309, p. 36.

[3]Finney, Charles. Attributes of Love. (Minneapolis, Min.,Bethany Fellowship, Inc., 1963).

[4]Vine's, Vol. 1, p. 218.

[5]Ibid, Vol. 2, p. 283.

[6]Ibid, Vol. 3, p. 168,169.

Christ Unlimited — P.O. Box 850 — Dewey, AZ 86327   USA

Lesson

[Author's Note: This lesson has material from the book, <u>The True God</u> and from the expository introduction. The answers are at the end of the workbook and do not have to be the exact wording given. The student simply needs to make sure that he, or she, has caught the concept or principle involved in the answer from the Word of God.]

I. The Image of God

A. Write a brief description of God.

_____

_____

_____

1. People's description of God will _____, according to:

a. _____

b. _____

c. _____

d. _____

2. Descriptions of God vary as we _____.

3. What is the major characteristic of God that is manifested over and over in His Word? _____
References: John 3:16; 1 John 4:16,19

B. How can we come to a true knowledge of God?

_____

1. What is the first discovery we need to make when we study the Word of God to understand Him better?

_____

2. Whose life can we study to get a better picture of God?

_____

II. The Image of God in Jesus
   A. What four specific books in the Bible can we read to learn about the life of Jesus while on earth?

   1. _____

Christ Unlimited — P.O. Box 850 — Dewey, AZ 86327   USA

2. _____

3. _____

4. _____

B. To truly see Jesus, we must:

1. Have our spiritual eyes opened and be _____.

That which is born of the flesh is flesh; and that which is born of
the Spirit is spirit. Marvel not that I said unto thee, Ye must be
born again.

John 3:6,7

2. See God's love for us through the sacrificial death of:

_____.

Reference: John 3:16-18

C. After we receive Jesus, then we are to grow in Him in order to
become like Him. Not only are we born again, but within us
now is the potential to become like the _____
Son of our new Father.

Christ Unlimited — P.O. Box 850 — Dewey, AZ 86327   USA

For whom he did foreknow, he also did predestinate to be conformed to the image of his Son, that he might be the firstborn among many brethren.

Romans 8:29

1. The most important factor after rebirth is to keep the right heart attitude before the Father. This means that we must daily:

   a. _____

   b. _____

   c. _____

2. Things that can hinder our conforming to the image of Jesus, excluding those above are:

   a. _____

   b. _____

   c. _____

   d. _____

3. Four concepts that determine whether a believer walks in victory as Jesus did are:

a. _____

b. _____

c. _____

d. _____

III. How To Live a Victorious Life

A. What are the three revelations necessary to have a victorious Christian walk?

1. First, we must know <u>who</u> _____ is.

a. God is _____.

Reference: . . . **God is love (1 John 4:8).**

(1) List four major Greek words and their meanings that are translated as one word, love, in English.

(a) _____

(b) _____

(c) _____

(d) _____

b. Other attributes of God include (name at least five and give a scripture for each):

(1) _____

(2) _____

(3) _____

(4) _____

(5) _____

References:

Isaiah 9:6; Psalm 136; James 1:5, 3:13-17;

Romans 11:33; Proverbs 3:19; Matthew 28:18; Acts

1:8; Psalm 86:15; John 14:6; Gal. 5:22,23;

1 Corinthians 14:33; Romans 15:5

c. Name one attribute that is not customarily associated with Deity:

_____

But I fear, lest by any means, as the serpent beguiled Eve through his subtilty so your minds should be corrupted from the simplicity that is in Christ.

                                        2 Corinthians 11:3

2. The second revelation we must have to begin living a victorious life is to know who we are_____.

    a. Who does the Bible say is righteous? _____

...There is none righteous, no, not one.

                                        Romans 3:10

    b. _____ works will not gain salvation for us, nor will _____ works keep us from God. Our works are simply a reflection of where we are in Christ.

Not by works of righteousness which we have done, but according to his mercy he saved us, by the washing of regeneration, and renewing of the Holy Ghost; Which he shed on us abundantly through Jesus Christ our Saviour.

                                        Titus 3:5,6

    (1) What one thing determines our place in God?

    _____

(2) Who are we apart from Christ? _____

(3) Who is our one example to follow in life?

_____

3. The third revelation necessary for a victorious life is to

know who we are _____ , or who He is _____.

a. Who are we in Christ Jesus?

_____

But as many as received him, to them gave he the power to become the sons of God, even to them that believe on his name.

John 1:12

Other References: 2 Peter 1:4-11

b. Because we have partaken of the divine nature of God through Christ (2 Pet. 1:4), we have the power to be _____ of all things, as Jesus was.

Reference:

Ye are of God, little children, and have overcome them: because greater is he (the Holy Spirit) that is in you, than he (the devil) that is in the world.

                                                              1 John 4:4

      c. Considering all of this, what is our destiny?

      (1) To be _____

...That ye, being rooted and grounded in love, May be able to comprehend with all saints what is the breadth, and length, and depth, and height; And to know the love of Christ, which passeth knowledge, that ye might be filled with all the fulness of God.

                                                     Ephesians 3:17-19

      (2) And, to _____

He that overcometh shall inherit all things; and I will be his God, and he shall be my son.

                                                     Revelation 21:7

      (3) What are the main characteristics of God that will make us perfect according to the verse below?

_____

Christ Unlimited — P.O. Box 850 — Dewey, AZ 86327   USA

Knowing this, that the trying of your faith worketh patience. But let patience have her perfect work, that ye may be perfect and entire, wanting nothing.

James 1:3,4

Christ Unlimited — P.O. Box 850 — Dewey, AZ 86327   USA

Overcoming Life Memory Verses

The suggested memory verses for this lesson are:

For whom he did foreknow, he also did predestinate to be conformed to the image of his Son, that he might be the firstborn among many brethren.

Romans 8:29

Beloved, let us love one another: for love is of God; and everyone that loveth is born of God, and knoweth God. He that loveth not knoweth not God; for God is love.

1 John 4:7,8

Christ Unlimited — P.O. Box 850 — Dewey, AZ 86327   USA

Christ Unlimited — P.O. Box 850 — Dewey, AZ 86327   USA

Review Outline

I. **We Can Really Know God**

A. We know Him by:

1. Turning to Him with our whole hearts, becoming born again

2. Studying the life of Jesus

3. Revelation through the Holy Spirit, who:

a. Reveals the Word to us.

b. Reveals Jesus to us.

c. Gives us an intimate picture of God.

d. Teaches us of God's love.

B. We can know Jesus by:

1. Studying the prophecies predicted of Messiah in the Old Testament.

2. Studying the life He lived on earth as revealed in the four gospels.

a. He was all-man as well as all-God and understands the human condition, because He lived it as child and adult.

b. He identifies with us at our present levels.

3. Studying the principles and concepts attributed to His teachings by the other New Testament writers.

C. We can only know God or Jesus through our spiritual eyes.

II. **Sonship With the Father Begins With the New Birth**

A. Jesus is the only Way to the Father.

1. Believe on Him with your whole heart

2. Confess Him with your mouth.

Christ Unlimited — P.O. Box 850 — Dewey, AZ 86327   USA

3. Forsake wickedness.

4. The Spirit of Christ reproduces His life within us.

5. Abiding in Him produces fruit.

   a. We have the potential to be like Him.

   b. Obedience produces the fruit of His character

B. Jesus calls us all to service

1. We must do works of the spirit and not the flesh.

2. Obedience brings rewards.

3. We must learn to recognize His voice when He calls.

4. Cleansing and training should precede active ministry.

   a. Everyone is called to pray.

   b. Everyone is called to witness of Jesus to others.

C. Jesus calls us to grow in Him.

1. Spiritual growth parallels natural growth.

2. Applying the Word of God in our lives causes spiritual growth.

3. Godly character is a prerequisite to exercising spiritual authority.

   a. Character is developed, not born in us.

   b. Godly character comes from conforming to the image of Jesus.

4. The Holy Spirit will teach us God's ways.

D. Jesus is the Prince of Peace

1. There is no peace apart from God.

2. Peace is a fruit of the Spirit.

3. Peace comes from keeping our minds fixed on God.

4. We are called to be peacemakers in the world.

Christ Unlimited — P.O. Box 850 — Dewey, AZ 86327   USA

5. We are to experience the peace of Jesus.

III. Becoming Like Our Father Requires Knowing His Character

A. The greatest attribute of our heavenly Father is <u>love</u>.

　　1. Love is His motive for sending Jesus to earth.

　　2. Love is His motive for forgiving us when we fail and repent.

B. Among His names, which tell us His nature, are Counsellor, Wonderful, Mighty God, and Everlasting Father.

　　1. He is good and perfect in every way.

　　2. Everything good and perfect comes from Him.

C. He is unlimited and infinite in every way.

　　1. He is not responsible for evil.

　　　　a. Sin originated with Lucifer.

　　　　b. All evil comes from our choosing to sin.

D. He has provided help for us in every area, including:

　　1. Salvation, through Jesus, by which we gain these things:

　　　　a. A new spirit

　　　　b. Healing and deliverance for the spirit, soul, and body

　　　　c. Renewing of the mind

　　　　d. Eternal life with God

　　2. He gives us counsel and empowerment through the Holy Spirit

　　　　a. We are told in the Bible to seek godly counsel from other believers.

　　　　　　(1) Demonic harassment comes many times from seeking wrong counsel.

　　　　　　(2) God gives the five-fold ministry for godly counsel.

b. The gifts of the Spirit give us guidance and hope.

c. He reveals root causes of our problems so correction can follow.

(1) Many of our problems result from lack of faith.

(2) Chains of iniquity also cause root problems.

d. He changes us into the image of Jesus, if we let Him.

3. God gives us knowledge and understanding through His Word.

4. He meets our needs through faith.

5. He helps, comforts, loves, and cares for us through His Holy Spirit.

IV. Levels of Spiritual Growth

A. Those at Babyhood/Childhood level:

1. Will act immature as natural babies or children do.

2. Will get into trouble more often through impulsiveness or lack of knowledge.

3. Will need much love, forgiveness, and prayer.

B. Those at teenage level:

1. Will think they know more than their "elders."

2. Will need help channeling their activities properly.

C. Mature Christians, God's ultimate intention for all of us:

1. Will grow into "fatherhood" in the Body and shepherd the lambs.

2. Will battle in the Spirit for the sheep.

3. Will manifest the nature and character of the heavenly Father by conforming to the image of Jesus.

4. Will judge no one after the flesh

    (Gender or race is not relevant in the Kingdom of God.)

5. Will recognize the spiritual ages of others.

D. Natural age is not an indicator of spiritual maturity.

V. How We Grow to Maturity

A. Essentials for Growth

1. Bible study

2. Daily prayer

3. Fellowship with other believers

4. Submission and obedience

    a. Disobedience opens the door to the enemy.

    b. Submission is a heart attitude.

5. Right heart attitudes

6. Continual repentance

B. Hindrances to growth

1. Mistaking Satan's work for God's

2. Ignorance of the Word

3. Misunderstanding the truth about chastening

    a. God chastises through His Word and through conviction
       from the Holy Spirit.

4. Attacks from Satan

C. Revelation in three areas:

1. Who God is

    a. Requires a balanced understanding of Scripture

    b. Requires knowledge of the central themes of the Bible

       (1) God's love

Christ Unlimited — P.O. Box 850 — Dewey, AZ 86327   USA

(2) Jesus' sacrificial death for our sins

(3) God's forgiveness and offer of abundant life

2. Who we are apart from Him (Rom. 3:10)

a. Our old natures are sinful.

b. We are unclean before the Lord.

c. Our righteousness is as filthy rags.

3. Who we are in Him

a. Empowered by the Holy Spirit (1 John 4:4)

b. Overcomers (Phil. 4:13)

VI. God's Ultimate Desire for His Children

A. Progressive intimacy with Him

B. Full enjoyment of His blessings

C. Fruitful service in sharing the Good News

Christ Unlimited — P.O. Box 850 — Dewey, AZ 86327   USA

Review Outline Quiz

1. What is the first step to knowing God?

_____

2. What is essential to our becoming like our heavenly Father?

_____

3. Who is our model in the Christian life?

_____

4. Which believers are called to witness to others and to pray?

_____

5. What is the prerequisite for the effective exercise of spiritual authority?

_____

6. Levels of spiritual growth parallel what other kind of growth?

_____

7. Is an older person automatically more spiritual than a younger?
   Why, or why not?

   _____

   _____

   _____

8. How does God chasten His children?

   _____

   _____

9. Can any human being be good in his, or her, own right?

   _____

   _____

10. What is God's ultimate goal for His children?

   _____

   _____

Christ Unlimited — P.O. Box 850 — Dewey, AZ 86327   USA

What You Need to Know About
Christ Unlimited Ministries

Purpose and Vision

Go ye therefore, and teach all nations, baptizing them in the name of the Father, and of the Son, and of the Holy Ghost: Teaching them to observe all things whatsoever I have commanded you: and, lo, I am with you always, even unto the end of the world. Amen.

Matthew 28:19, 20

CHRIST UNLIMITED is not "another denomination," sect, or just a separate group. It is an arm of the Body of Christ — the Church of Jesus Christ, which has been called to strengthen the Body at large. We also believe we have been called to help establish the Kingdom of God in the earth.

CHRIST UNLIMITED is open to help and work with all Bible-believing Christians regardless of their church or denominational affiliations and committed to helping wherever possible in evangelistic and teaching outreaches.

CHRIST UNLIMITED believes that time is running out and the Gospel has not been preached to every creature. Many nations have not heard the Gospel, and in many places, doors for evangelism are closing. We believe it is time all Christians cooperated with the Lord in breaking down denominational walls for a united front line against the kingdom of darkness and in setting up the Kingdom of the Lord Jesus Christ by the power of the Holy Spirit.

CHRIST UNLIMITED provides such tools as to enable the saints of God to establish the Kingdom of God in the earth. We encourage groups of prayer warriors who will pray, fast, and intercede for the nations. This, we believe, is weapon number one. We teach believers how to overcome through spiritual warfare and through knowing how to use their authority in Christ Jesus through the Word and the power of the Holy Spirit.

Christians need to know how to bring down the forces of darkness in their own lives and in the lives of those to whom they minister. We provide such tools as Bibles, literature, CHRIST UNLIMITED books, and downloadable audio and video. We promote the Gospel going forth via any means of communication, including radio and video, the INTERNET, and literature. We promote teaching seminars, Bible schools, and correspondence courses, all aimed at winning souls to Christ and building the Body of Christ into maturity.

Bud and Betty Miller serve the Lord together as founders of the multi-vision ministry outreach, CHRIST UNLIMITED. The outreaches of this ministry have stemmed from a tremendous desire to see the Word of God taught in its balanced entirety. The Millers are firm believers in prayer and, through prayer, have seen many released from the bondages of fear, failure, and defeat.

Christ Unlimited — P.O. Box 850 — Dewey, AZ 86327 USA

The Millers have a world-wide vision for spreading the full-gospel message and teaching God's Word. Bud not only preaches and pastors a church, but is director of **CHRIST UNLIMITED PUBLISHING**, an outreach dedicated to publishing God's Word in many languages. His experience, openness to the Holy Spirit, and down-to-earth expression of God's love has blessed many. God has endowed Betty with a rare gift of teaching that makes her a practical and effective "handmaiden of the Lord." Both Bud and Betty have hearts turned toward evangelism and missions, desiring to tell everyone of God's wonderful love. Their anointed teaching comes across with simplicity and in the power of the Holy Spirit.

The outreaches of **CHRIST UNLIMITED** are in obedience to the words of our Lord in Mark 16:15: **Go ye into all the world and preach the gospel to every creature.** This mandate from the Lord presents a challenge to our generation as an estimated 25 percent of the world's population still have not heard the Good News of Jesus Christ.[1]

CHRIST UNLIMITED MINISTRIES also is dedicated to teaching God's Word. Hosea 4:6 says: **My people are destroyed for lack of knowledge.** Many Christians are leading defeated lives simply because they do not know God's Word in its fullest.

CHRIST UNLIMITED MINISTRIES has provided literature for those who desire to know God's Word in a greater way. The main thrust of the teaching and literature is directed at "How to be an overcomer." In the endtimes, we must be prepared to overcome the onslaughts of Satan. Many Christians are suffering needlessly because they do not know how to overcome sickness, depression, divorce, fear, and financial failure. **CHRIST UNLIMITED MINISTRIES** provides answers for troubled families as well as trains workers for service.

DOCTRINAL STATEMENT

> Jesus answered them, and said, My doctrine is not mine, but his that sent me. If any man will do his will, he shall know of the doctrine, whether it be of God or whether I speak of myself.
> John 7:16,17

Inspiration of Scriptures: We believe that the Holy Bible is he written Word of the Living God. We believe it was inspired by the Holy Spirit and recorded by holy men of old. It is infallible in content and a perfect treasure of heavenly instruction which is truth without any mixture of error. The Bible reveals the principles by which God will judge us and reveals His great plan of salvation. It will remain eternally. We believe the Bible is the true center of Christian union and the supreme standard by which all human conduct, creeds, and opinions should be tried. Therefore, we believe this Word should go into all the world and should be given first place in every believer's life (2 Tim. 3:16; Heb. 4:12; 1 Pet. 1:23-25; and 2 Pet. 1:19-21).

God: We believe in one God revealed in three persons: the Father, the Son, and the Holy Ghost . . . making up the blessed Trinity (Matt. 3:16,17; 1 John 5:6,7).

Man: We believe that man, in his natural state, is a sinner — lost, undone, without hope, and without God (Rom. 3:19-23; Gal. 3:22; Eph. 2:1,2-12).

Salvation: We believe the terms of salvation are repentance toward God for sin and a personal, heartfelt faith in the Lord Jesus Christ. This will result in a new birth. Salvation is possible only through God's grace, not by our works. Works are simply the fruit of
salvation (Acts 3:19,20; Rom. 4:1-5, 5:1; Eph. 2:8-10).

Body of Christ: We believe the Body of Christ is made up of all who have been born again regardless of denominational differences. We believe in the spirit of unity, while allowing for variety in individual ministries as to their work, calling, and location as directed by the Holy Spirit (Acts 10:34,35; 1 Cor. 12:12-31).

Blood Atonement: We believe in the saving power of the blood of Jesus and His imputed righteousness (Acts 4:12; Rom. 4:1-9, 5:1-11; Eph. 1:3-14).

Bodily Resurrection: We believe in the bodily resurrection of Jesus Christ (Luke 24:39-43; John 20:24-29).

Ascension: We believe that Christ Jesus ascended to the Father and is presently engaged in building a place for us in Heaven and interceding for the saints (John 14:2,3; Rom. 8:34).

Second Coming: We believe in the visible, bodily return of Christ Jesus to this earth, to meet His Church (Bride) and to judge the world (Acts 1:10,11; 1 Thess. 4:13-18; 2 Thess. 1:7-10; James 5:8; Rev. 1:7).

Ordinances: We believe that the two ordinances of the Body of Christ are water baptism and the Lord's Supper (Matt. 28:19; 1 Cor. 11:24-26).

Heaven and Hell: We believe Scripture clearly sets forth the doctrines of eternal punishment for the lost and eternal bliss and service for the saved — a literal hell for the unsaved and heaven for the saved (Matt. 25:34,41,46; Luke 16:19-31; John 14:1-3; Rev. 20:11-15).

Holy Spirit: We believe the Holy Spirit to be the third person of the Trinity whose purpose in the redemption of man is to convict of sin, regenerate the repentant believer, guide the believer into all truth, indwell all believers, and give gifts to those He wills that they may minister as Christ would to men. We believe that the manifestations of the Holy Spirit recorded in 1 Corinthians 12:8-11 will operate through present-day Christians who yield to Jesus (Luke 11:13; John 7:37-39, 14:16,17, 16:7-14; Acts 2:1-18).

We believe the baptism in the Holy Spirit, with the evidence of speaking in other tongues as the Spirit gives utterance, is for all believers as promised by John the Baptist (Matt. 3:11), Jesus (Acts 1:4-8), and Peter (Acts 2:38-41). The fulfillment of this promise was witnessed by early disciples of Christ (Acts 2:4, 10:44-47, 19:1-6) and operates in many present-day disciples of the Lord Jesus Christ.

Christ Unlimited — P.O. Box 850 — Dewey, AZ 86327   USA

<u>Divine Healing:</u> We believe God has used doctors, medicines, and other natural means of healing; however, we believe divine healing is provided for believers in the atonement made by Jesus' blood shed on the cross (Isa. 53:5; 1 Pet. 2:24). We believe divine healing may be appropriated by the laying on of hands by the elders (James 5:14-16), by the prayer of an anointed person gifted by the Holy Spirit for healing the sick (1 Cor. 12:9), or by a direct act of receiving this provision by faith (Mark 11:23,24).

MINISTRY FINANCING

> But seek ye first the kingdom of God, and his righteousness; and all these things shall be added unto you.
> Matthew 6:33

We want to share with readers the instructions the Lord gave us in regard to financing this ministry. As this is the Holy Spirit's work, we are to let Him speak to the hearts of people as to what and how much He wants them to give. Quite simply, we are to share the vision He has given us and trust Him to provide for all that we need. We believe the Lord pays for the things He orders, and if He does not order something, we do not want to engage in it. Pray with us that we will stay close to the Lord, and that, in seeking His righteousness, we will be able to hear His instructions clearly as to what He desires us to do. If we do that, we know we shall never lack of the things needed to do His work.

CHRIST UNLIMITED MINISTRIES, INC. is a tax-exempt 501(c)(3) non-profit church, established locally in the , Arizona area.

[1]Barrett, David B. <u>Cosmos, Chaos, and Gospel</u> (Birmingham: New Hope Publishers, 1987), p. 75.

FOR ADDITIONAL STUDY

This book is taken from a course of Bible Studies called the Overcoming Life Series. The entire series is a virtual "spiritual tool chest," as it covers a multitude of subjects every Christian faces in his walk with God. It also answers questions that many believers have concerning the current move of God. These are dealt with in a balanced approach and in the light of the Scripture. God's people are not to live fustrated, defeated lives, but rather they are to be victorious overcomers! Other books available with their companion workbooks are:

PROVE ALL THINGS – Christ warned that great deception would be one of the signs of the end times. In this book, instruction is given on how to recognize false prophets and teachings. Clear Scriptural guidelines are given on discerning the Spirit of truth versus the spirit of error. The book deals with how to judge without being judgmental.

THE TRUE GOD - This is a teaching on the character of God, explaining why God does certain things, and why it is against His nature to do other things. It differentiates between the things for which God is responsible and the things for which the devil is responsible. Our responsibility as Christians destined to overcome is made clear so that we can live victorious lives.

THE WILL OF GOD - This lesson teaches us not only how to know the will of God in our personal lives, family, ministry and finances, but also brings understanding as to why God allows sin, sickness and suffering in the world. As overcomers, Chritians are not to suffer under many of the things we have accepted as normal.

KEYS TO THE KINGDOM - Instruction on how to gain authority in God's Kingdom through prayer is the topic of this book. Many principles and methods of prayer are covered, such as praying in the Spirit, fasting and prayer, travailing prayer, praise, intercession and spiritual warfare.

EXPOSING SATAN'S DEVICES - This book is a powerful expose' of Satan's tricks, tactics and lies. Cult and Occultic methods and groups are listed so Christians can detect their activity. Demon activity is discussed and deliverance and casting out demons is dealt with in detail. Satan's kingdom is uncovered and the Christian is taught to overcome through spiritual discernment and warfare.

HEALING OF THE SPIRIT, SOUL AND BODY - This book teaches how to overcome emotional problems, as well as physical ones, and how to receive divine healing. It also teaches how to renew the carnal mind and walk in the spirit of life, thereby overcoming depression, loneliness and fear.

NEITHER MALE NOR FEMALE - What is the woman's role in the church and home? Who is a woman's spiritual head and covering? Does God call women to the five-fold ministry? What does God's Word say about divorce, celibacy and choosing a marriage partner? These and other woman related topics are Scripturally examined.

EXTREMES OR BALANCE? - Many Christians have hurt the cause of Christ through "out-of-balance" teachings and demonstrations. This book shows how to avoid those areas. It also deals wisely with the excesses and extremes in the body of Christ.

THE PATHWAY INTO THE OVERCOMER'S WALK - This book contains answers to the questions an overcomer faces as he presses toward the prize of the high calling in Christ Jesus. How can we be conformed to the image of Christ? How does the Holy Spirit work with the overcomers in the end times? What are the overcomer's rewards? Please visit our website for information on how to order the complete "Overcoming Life Bible Study." We also have electronic books and a condensed Bible School on-line at: www.BibleResources.org

Christ Unlimited — P.O. Box 850 — Dewey, AZ 86327   USA

<u>Divine Healing:</u> We believe God has used doctors, medicines, and other natural means of healing; however, we believe divine healing is provided for believers in the atonement made by Jesus' blood shed on the cross (Isa. 53:5; 1 Pet. 2:24). We believe divine healing may be appropriated by the laying on of hands by the elders (James 5:14-16), by the prayer of an anointed person gifted by the Holy Spirit for healing the sick (1 Cor. 12:9), or by a direct act of receiving this provision by faith (Mark 11:23,24).

MINISTRY FINANCING

> But seek ye first the kingdom of God, and his righteousness; and all these things shall be added unto you.
>   Matthew 6:33

We want to share with readers the instructions the Lord gave us in regard to financing this ministry. As this is the Holy Spirit's work, we are to let Him speak to the hearts of people as to what and how much He wants them to give. Quite simply, we are to share the vision He has given us and trust Him to provide for all that we need. We believe the Lord pays for the things He orders, and if He does not order something, we do not want to engage in it. Pray with us that we will stay close to the Lord, and that, in seeking His righteousness, we will be able to hear His instructions clearly as to what He desires us to do. If we do that, we know we shall never lack of the things needed to do His work.

CHRIST UNLIMITED MINISTRIES, INC. is a tax-exempt 501(c)(3) non-profit church, established locally in the Dewey, Arizona area.

[1]Barrett, David B. <u>Cosmos, Chaos, and Gospel</u> (Birmingham: New Hope Publishers, 1987), p. 75.

The True God Workbook

Answers to Lesson and Quiz

Answers to Lesson

I. **The Image of God**
   A. A brief description of God could be something like this: Creator and sustainer of the entire universe, who is my dearest friend and greatest love, because He is love.

     1. Vary, or differ
       a. Knowledge of Him personally.
       b. Knowledge of His Word.
       c. Knowledge of Him through others.
       d. Knowledge of Him viewed through experiences.
     2. Mature, or grow in Him
     3. Love
   B. By seeking Him in His Book, the Bible
     1. There is only <u>one</u> God and <u>one</u> way to Heaven.
     2. Jesus

II. **The Image of God in Jesus**
   A.
     1. Matthew
     2. Mark
     3. Luke
     4. John
   B.
     1. Be born-again
     2. His Son, Jesus.
   C.
     1. Firstborn
     a. Pray
     b. Study God's Word
     c. Fellowship with like believers
     2.
     a. Disobedience
     b. Being unsubmissive or unyielding — rebellious
     c. Wrong attitudes
     d. Wrong ideas about God
     3.
     a. Our concept of God
     b. Our concept of Satan
     c. Our concept of self
     d. Our concept of others

Christ Unlimited — P.O. Box 850 — Dewey, AZ 86327   USA

III. How To Live a Victorious Life
    A. Three revelations necessary to a victorious walk are:
        1. Who <u>God</u> is.
            a. Love
                (1) <u>Agape</u> — Divine love
                (2) <u>Phileo</u> — Tender affection
                (3) <u>Philadelphia</u> — Brotherly love
                (4) <u>Eros</u> — Sexual love
            b. Attributes or characteristics
               The answers to 1-5 can be any of the list discussed in the expository
               introduction.
            c. Simplicity
        2. Without Him
            a. No human, only God
            b. Good, bad
                (1) A relationship with Jesus ("Being born again" also is an accept-
                    able answer.)
                (2) Nothing
                (3) Jesus
        3. In Him — in us
            a. Everything He is and sons of God.
            b. Overcomers
            c.
                (1) Filled with all of the fullness of God
                (2) Inherit all things
                (3) Faith and patience

Christ Unlimited — P.O. Box 850 — Dewey, AZ 86327   USA

Answers to Review Outline Quiz

1. Becoming born again
2. Knowing the nature and character of God
3. Jesus
4. All believers
5. Godly character
6. Natural growth
7. No. Spiritual age <u>parallels</u> natural growth in its progress from one level to another, but a 70-year-old who has just become born again is a "babe in Christ," whose spiritual growth has just begun.
8. God chastens His children through their reading of the Word and through the Holy Spirit's speaking or "witnessing" to our consciences.
9. No
10. Progressive intimacy with Him, full enjoyment of His blessings, and fruitful service in sharing the Good News and to be conformed to His image.

Christ Unlimited — P.O. Box 850 — Dewey, AZ 86327   USA

www.ingramcontent.com/pod-product-compliance
Lightning Source LLC
Chambersburg PA
CBHW081524040426

42447CB00013B/3335